**EYESIGHT AND PERCEPTION**

*The eye only does part of the job of seeing. It takes in light and turns it into something the brain can use. The rest of seeing happens in the brain, and in the final analysis perception involves the "mind", which is different from the eye or brain. For example, your mind is what tells you to turn your head away from something, or when to look. If your mind tells you to turn your head away from something that you don't want to see, then there is no direct way you can visually perceive it. There is an important philosophical question about whether the mind is part of, or not part of the body. The eye and brain, and the nervous system to which they are connected, are parts of the body. It is lucky that artists can do their work without answering the question "what is mind", or "how do we know?" In philosophy this enormous question is called epistemology. Our eyes select what we see in many ways. First by where our mind tells us to look, and next in what we are willing to accept (as when we see something so unusual we can't believe that we see it), and then in the fact that they are designed to see only part of the light that comes to them. We can't see the*



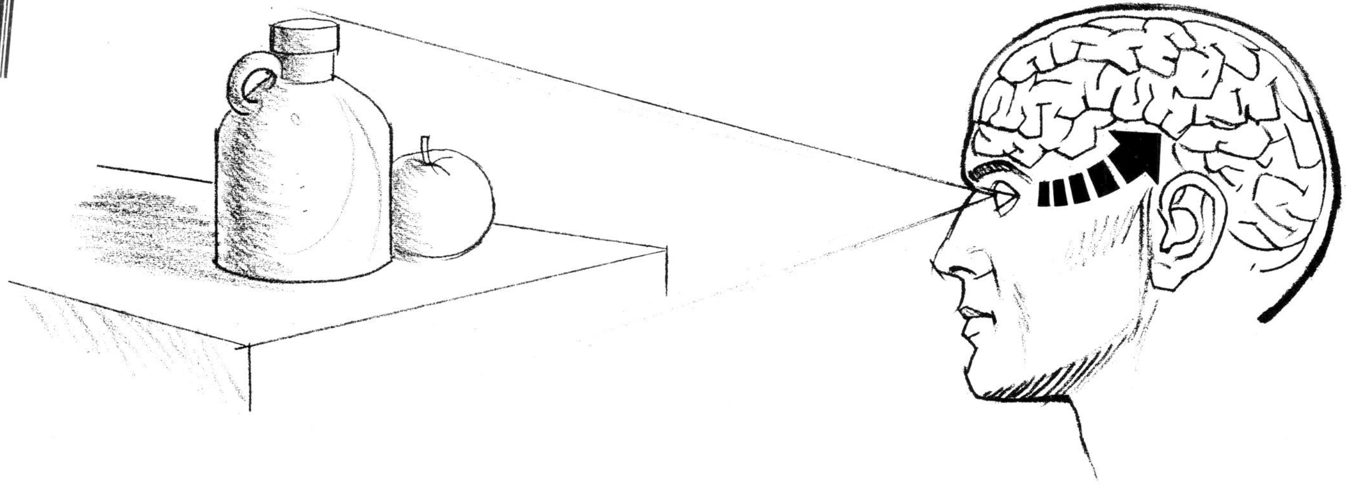

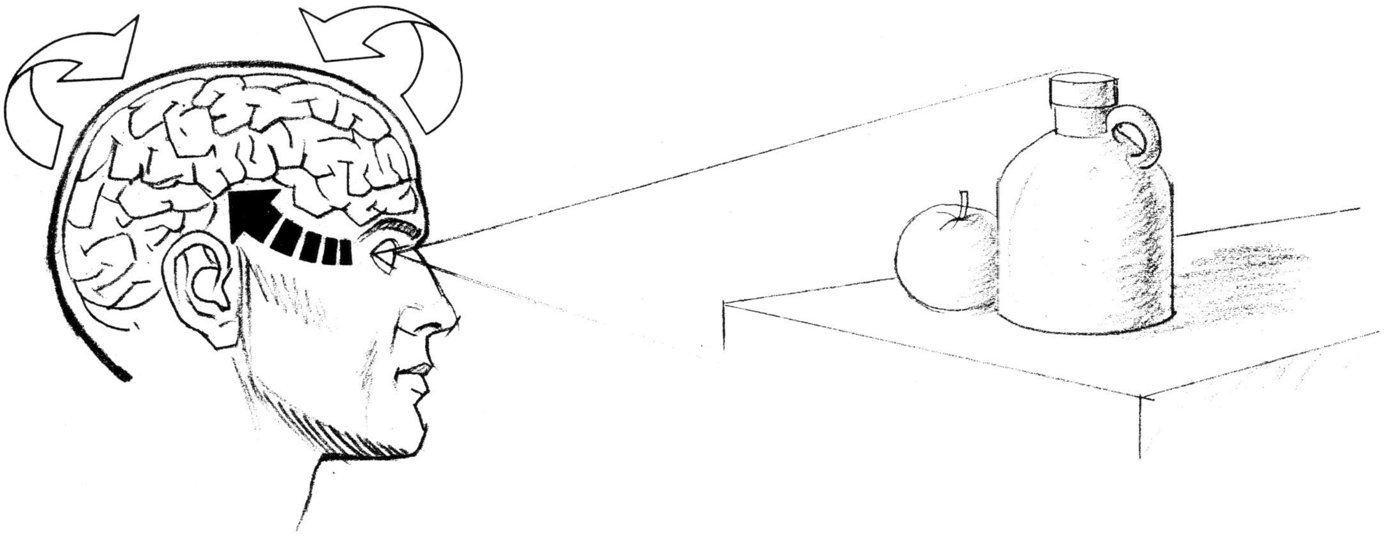

*kind of light that an x-ray machine puts out, nor the radiation of a "radio" station, because our eyes don't work that way. To make matters more interesting, we not only see things that are there, but sometimes we see things that are not there, even if we are not insane and hallucinating. When we dream, we see things that are not there, and we can remember or imagine things and the way they look when they are not around. The fact that artists can do so much with visual perception, when science has so many unanswered questions, makes visual perception and art very interesting things to study. We have two eyes. Nature didn't just decide to give us a spare. If you look at your finger ten inches from your nose, and close one eye after the other you can see the finger jump from left to right. That means when we look with both eyes open we're seeing from two directions at once, and seeing in three dimensions (length, width, and depth). This is called "binocular" (two-eyed) vision, and it helps us to locate things in space. This is part of the way we can judge the distance and volume of things.*

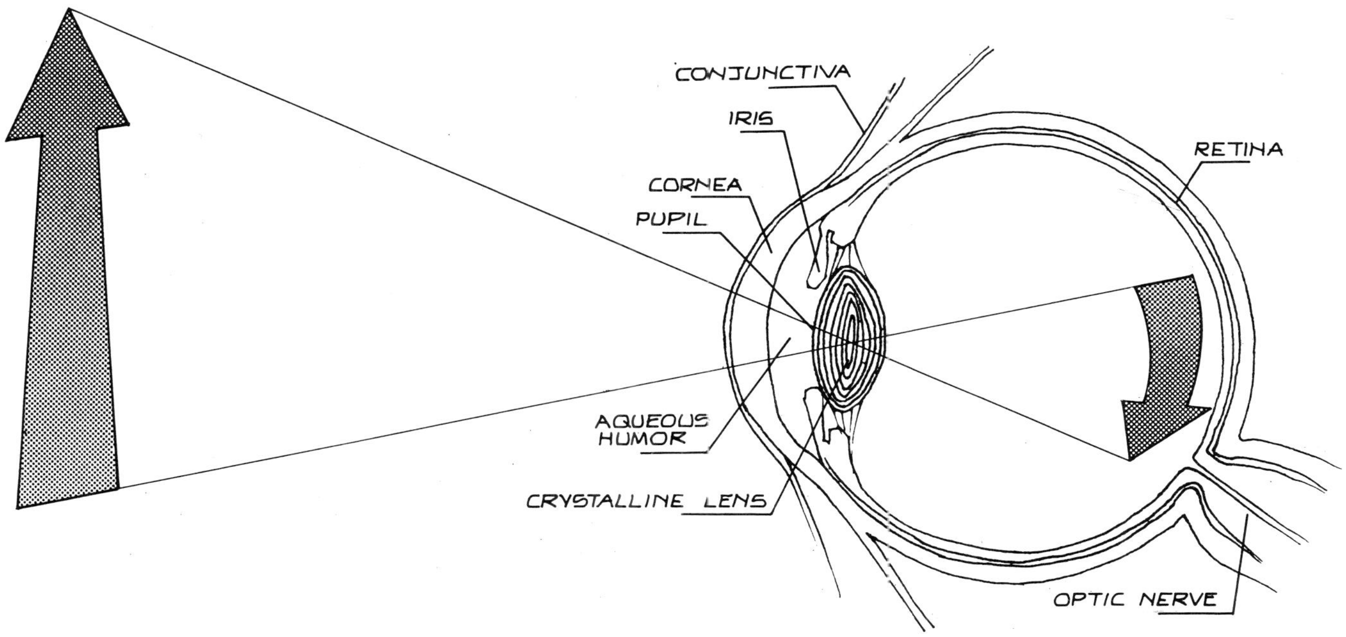

## THE OBJECT OF PERCEPTION

*The object of perception is anything which makes up, physically, the world in which we live, a world of shapes occupying space and reflecting light. Everything - men, plants, animals, utensils etc. - has a certain shape; and for the purposes of the picture, the "shape" is the first important item to be considered (1). The second item is the "composition", that is the relationship of position and dimensions between the various shapes (2). When we take a kettle, a bowl, a bottle, a glass and an apple, and we arrange them in a certain way on the table and so define a group, then we have a composition. Each element of such a group has and maintains, on the basis of its specific form, its own "tension", or an interplay of several tensions, as shown by the arrows (3), and the dynamics of these invisible forces is also a distinguishing item. Another item is "value", which means tones of grey, that is the gradation of intensity from white to black (4). Then we must consider "light", which can be direct or diffuse, strong or weak and which also has its own precise direction (5). Finally we have "space" (6), which is the part shown or the totality of an environment that our composition brings to life.*

1

2

3

4

5

6

**FORM - LINE - STROKE**

*By the word "form", we wish to define the exterior outlined shape of everything which takes up space, excluding for the moment all the other meanings with which the some word is used, both literal and metaphorical. This exterior aspect can be of a single object (the form of the object), or of a group of objects (configuration); but it must be borne in mind that we can only speak of real and proper " configuration" if the group is organized and has an order of its own. The most important elementary means for the drawing of forms is the "line".*

*The line is made by a certain type of "stroke", which can have a variety of characteristics such as soft, hard, jagged, broken, etc. For blocking in, chiaroscuro effects etc., the stroke can be multiplied in an infinite variety of arrangements. In this way we will get sections of parallel strokes, hatching strokes crossed at right or diagonal angles, areas which are almost merged together and areas where the strokes are separated from each other. All this can be with strokes which are delicate or incisive, slender or thick, according to our wishes, depending on the results we want to obtain.*

*To draw the forms, the line first defines the outline, putting a precise limit between the form and the space surrounding it, or between form and form, and it sketches only the minimum information necessary about what is inside the form to clarify the form itself.*

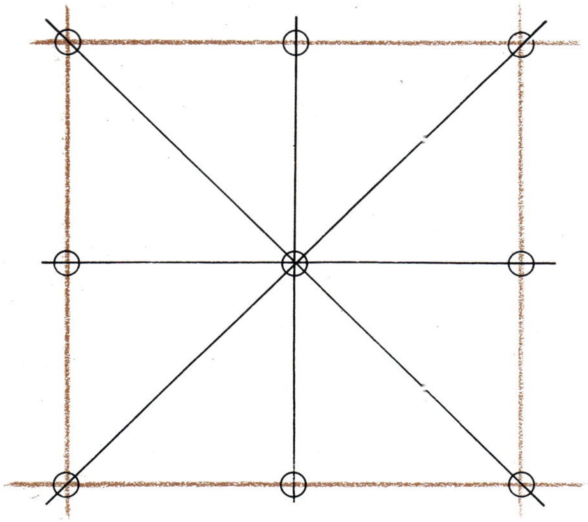

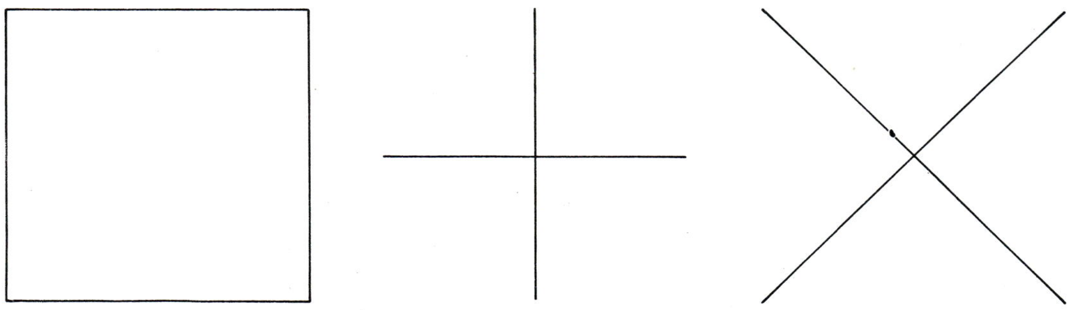

**STRUCTURE OF SHAPES AND FORMS - THE SQUARE**

*Shape is the two-dimensional object, and form is the appearance of the third dimension, depth. Examining the regular division of shapes and forms helps us to observe something about how space can be divided and subdivided.*

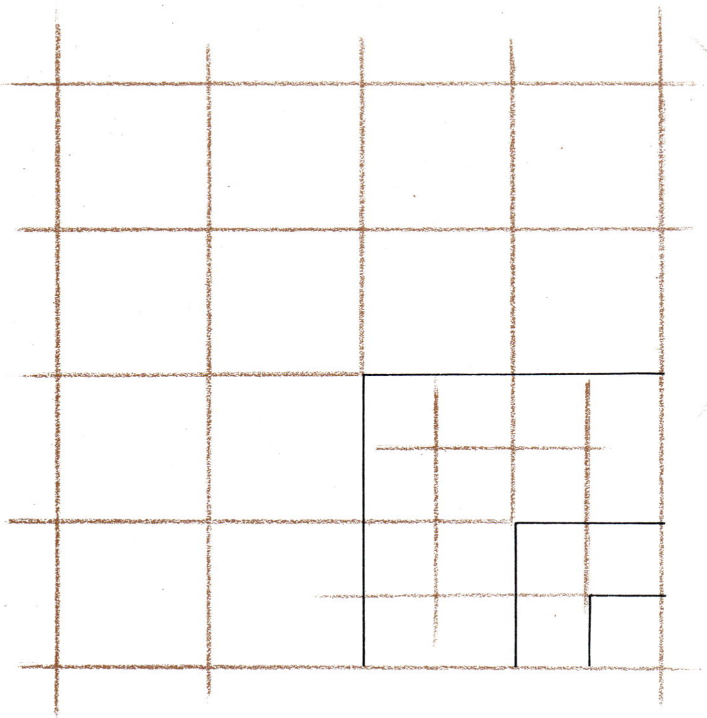

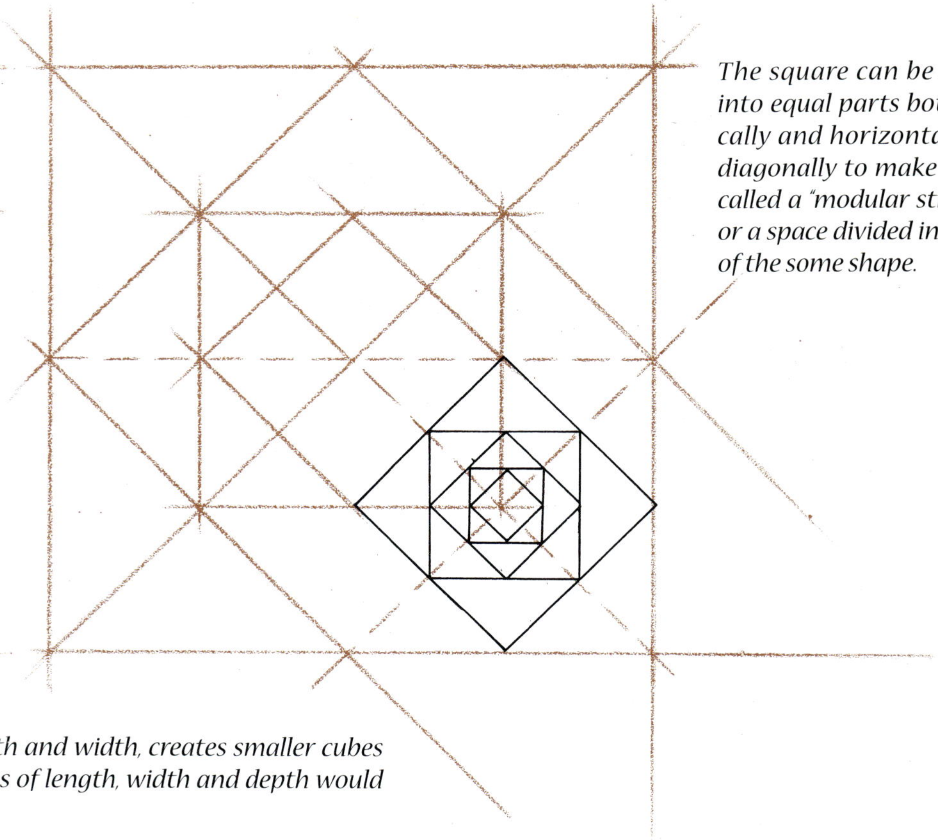

*The square can be divided into equal parts both vertically and horizontally, and diagonally to make what is called a "modular structure", or a space divided into parts of the some shape.*

**CUBE**

*Subdividing the cube, because it has depth as well as length and width, creates smaller cubes as the modules. Repeated division in half of the dimensions of length, width and depth would make smaller and smaller cubes as modules.*

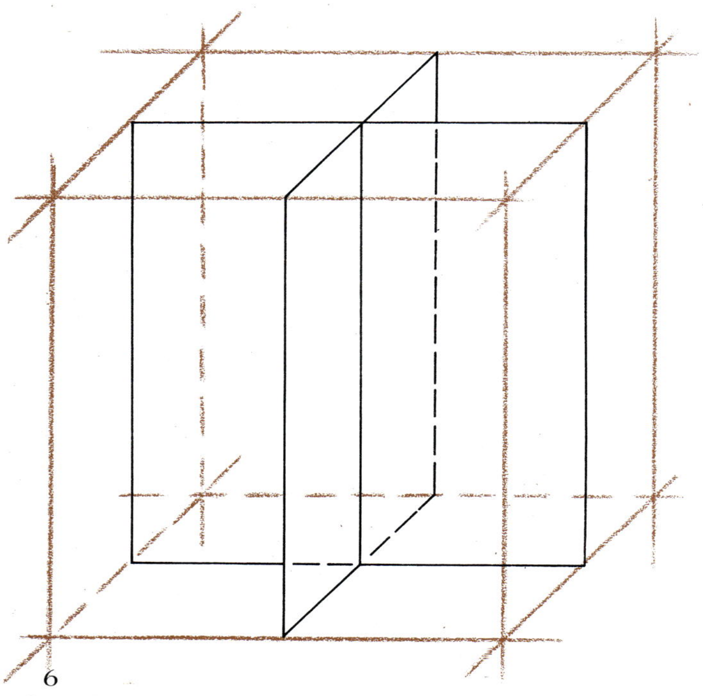

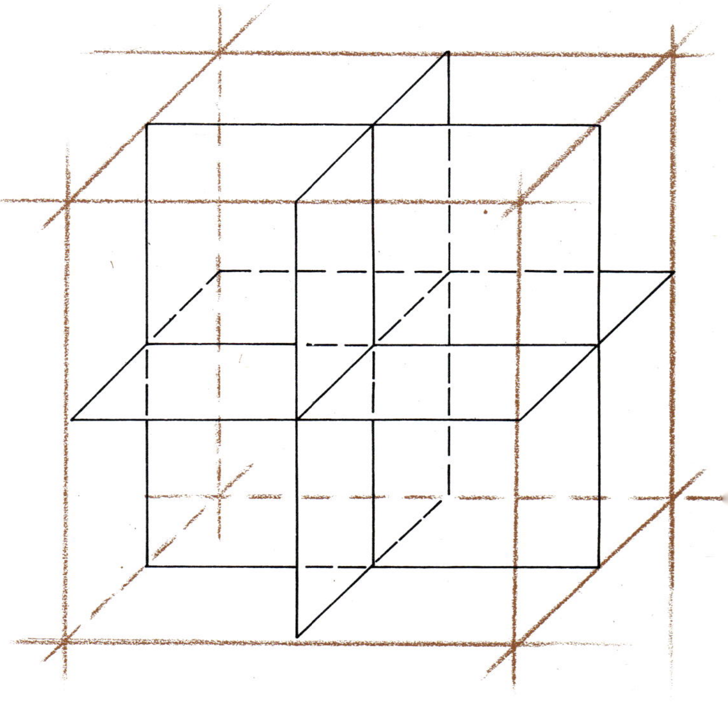

**CIRCLE AND SPHERE**

*Simple two-dimensional shapes like the circle have their three-dimensional equivalents, like the sphere. The circle can be divided by cutting it into equal wedges with radii, lines from the center to the rim. To divide the sphere, it has to be cut in the depth dimension in just the same way, with every radius meeting in the center, and being equally spaced around the outside.*

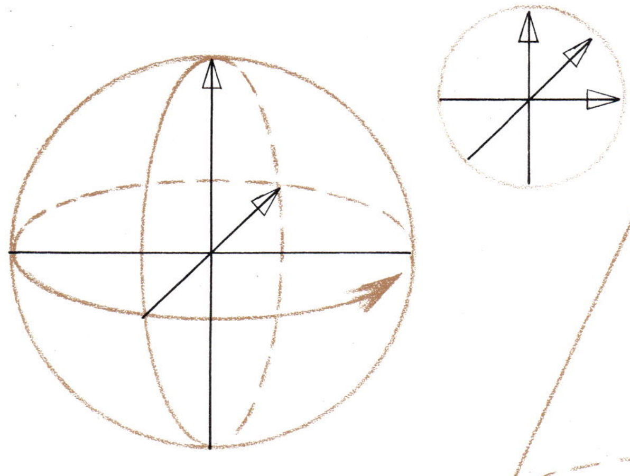

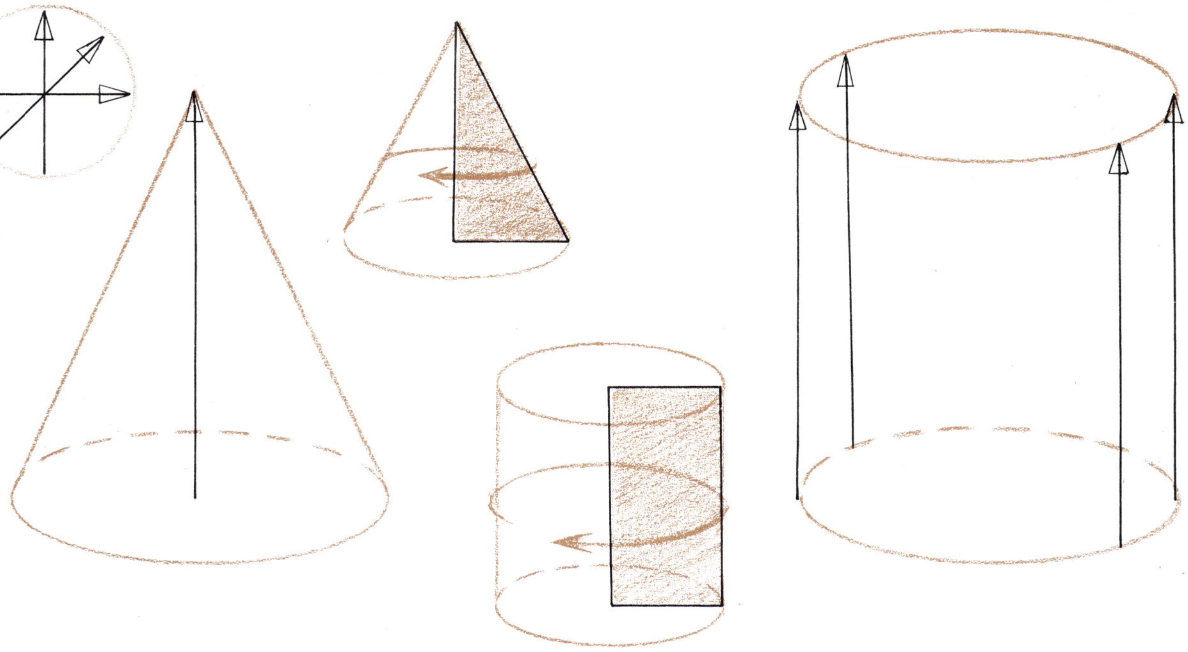

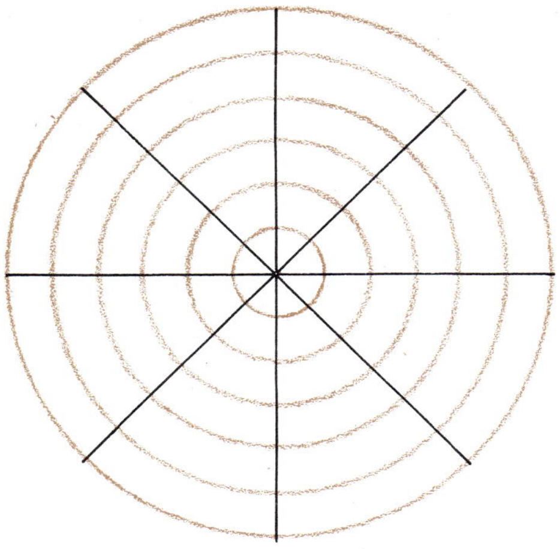

**CYLINDER AND CONE**

*Both the cylinder and the cone are three-dimensional. The cylinder can be seen as the rotation of a rectangle, and the cone as the rotation of a triangle. They both have circular bases, and can therefore be cut in the dimensions of length and width just the way a circle is. One method of division in depth would be to cut concentric vertical slices beginnning at each base.*

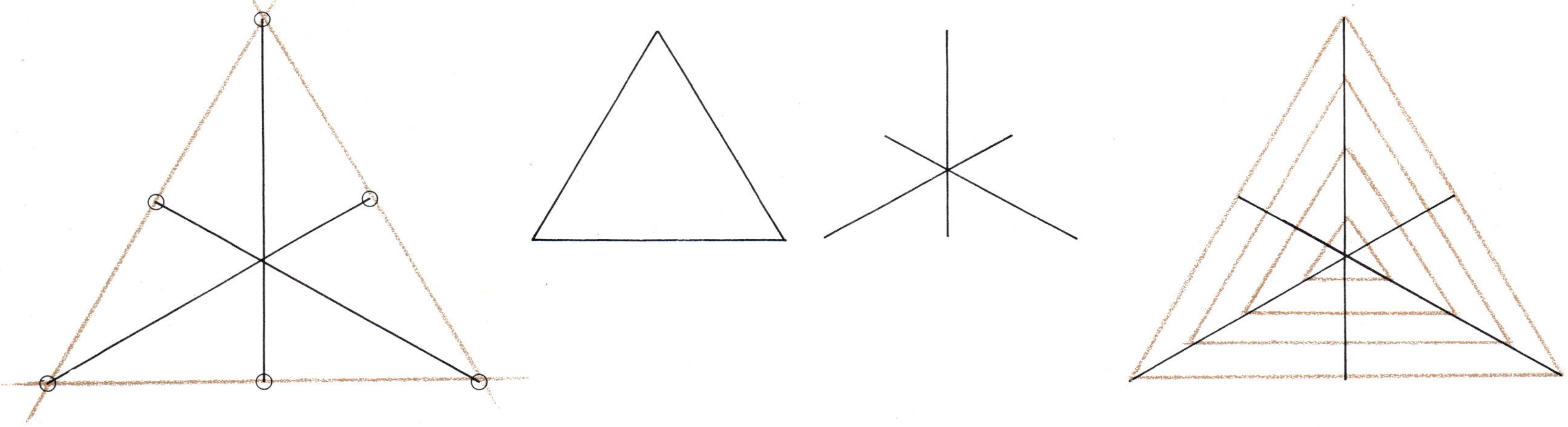

**EQUILATERAL TRIANGLE**

*The two-dimensional equilateral triangle, so called because every side is the same length, can be equally subdivided in several interesting ways. As above, which does not yield equal modules, or as to the right, which does.*

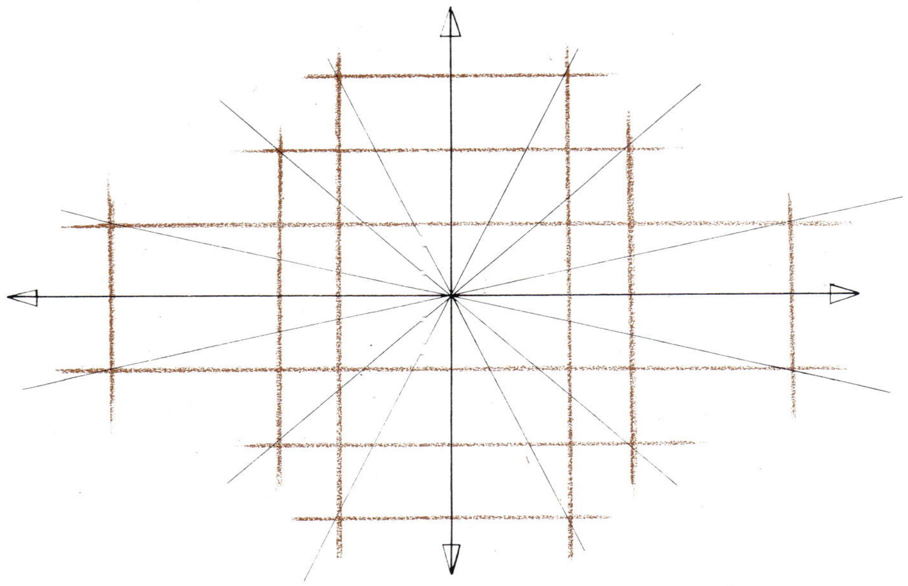

## RECTANGLE

*We conclude this rapid reference to the internal structure of simple geometric forms with the rectangle, which is one of the most interesting. If we center a series of rectangles on two perpendicular straight lines acting as medians, we observe that their diagonals never coincide: as we pass gradually from the tall, narrow rectangle to the lower, wider one, they give the impression of opening continually wider, and finally tending to coincide with the common horizontal median. If then our eye retraces its path, we see the diagonals gradually closing towards the vertical median. Likewise, the vertical median continues to get shorter while the horizontal median gets longer, and vice versa. It seems obvious that the rectangle, although based on the same internal structure as the square, has in addition its own "mobility" which makes it - especially in the figurative sense - a dynamic form.*

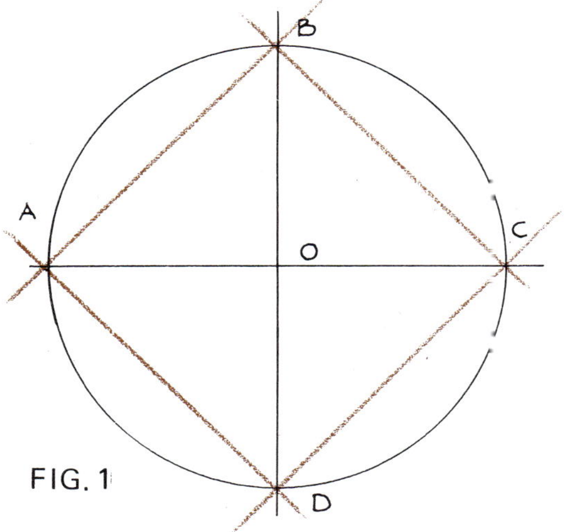


FIG. 1

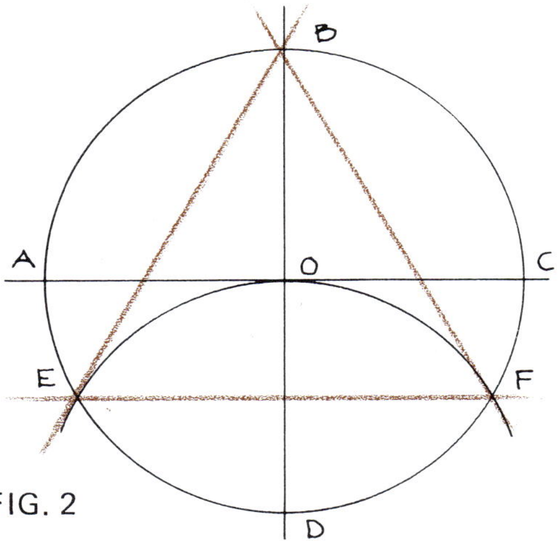


FIG. 2

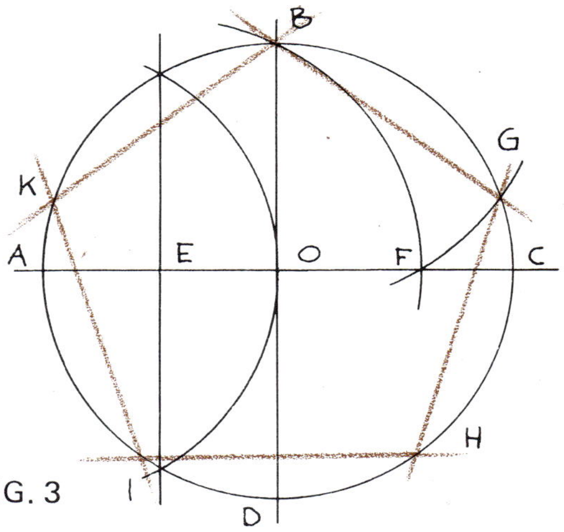


FIG. 3

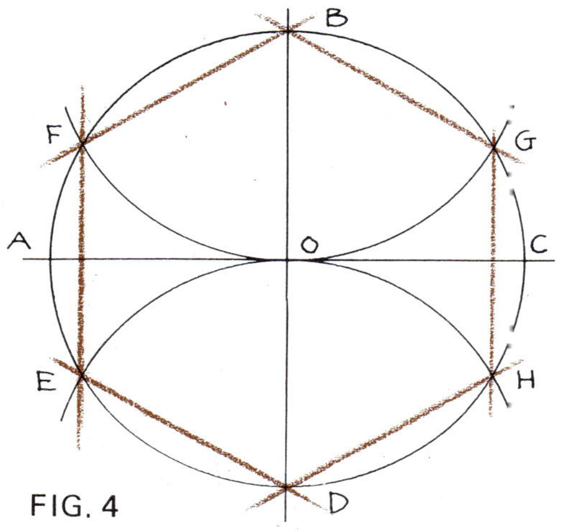


FIG. 4

## CONSTRUCTION OF SIMPLE FORMS

*Because the geometry of space division is often used as the basis for composition in art and design, it is important to have a grasp of these fundamentals. Here is shown the construction of regular polygons drawn inside a circle and of two types of ellipses, with ruler and compass.*

*FIG. 1 - The square is obtained by joining points A-B, B-C, C-D, D-A, which are the points of intersection on the circle of the two diameters perpendicular to each other.*

*FIG. 2 - The side E-F of the equilateral triangle is nothing more than the parallel of the diameter A-C, passing through the middle of the radius O-D; the other two sides are obtained by joining points E and F with B.*

*FIG. 3 - Putting the point of the compass on point E which divides radius O-A in two, an arc is drawn from E-B which bisects diameter A-C at F; then, putting the point on B, an arc is drawn from B-F bisecting the circle at G. The segment with the straight line B-G represents the side of the pentagon, and to have its base it is sufficient to repeat the aforesaid side from G-H, H-I, I-K, K-B.*

*FIG. 4 - For the hexagon, point the compass on D, with an opening equal to radius D-O, and bisect the circle at E and at H, then repeat the operation, putting the point on B and bisecting at F and G. The hexagon is the result of joining D with E, E with F, F with B, B with G, G with H and H with D.*

*FIG. 5 - Extending the sides of the equilateral triangle as in the figure, put the compass point on 1 and, with the compass open from 1-3, make the arc 3-A; then put the point on 2 and with the compass open from 2-A, make the arc A-B; then put the point on 3 with the compass open from 3-B for the arc B-C, and once more on 1 with the compass open from 1-C for the arc C-D and so on.*

*FIG. 6 - Proceed as for the spiral based on the triangle, pointing the compass on 1, opening it from 1-4 for the arc 4-A, on 2, opening it from 2-A for the arc A-B, on 3, opening it from 3-B for the arc B-C, and so on at will.*

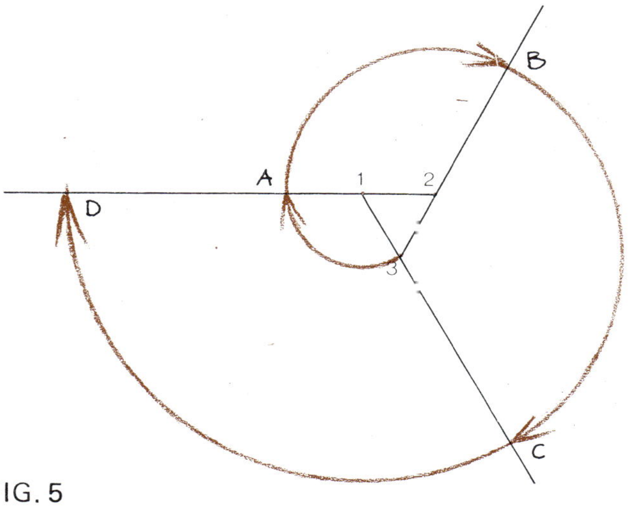


FIG. 5

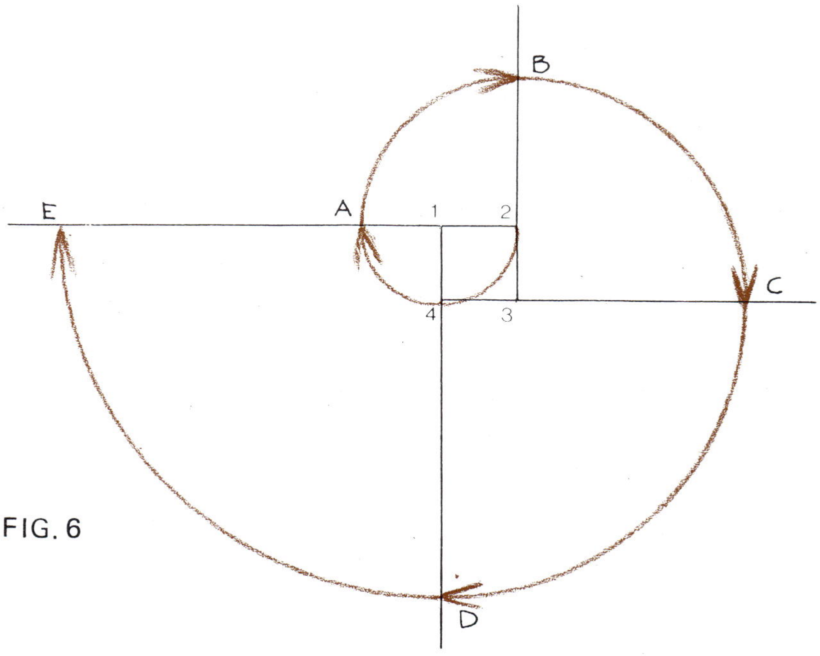


FIG. 6

**ENLARGEMENTS**

*The modular structure of square and rectangle can be used to create grids that aid in enlarging and reducing drawings and designs. This is also called "scaling". A grid drawn over the original is drawn proportionately larger or smaller on a blank surface. By closely observing and transferring the small parts of the drawing in each module to the new drawing, the proportions of the whole can be preserved. Naturally, the more drawing skill one has, the less one needs to divide the grid into small pieces. The pieces can be larger and larger as a person develops skill until it is either the edges of the drawing surface that are used for reference, or until one can use an imaginary grid and the relationships of shapes within the drawing for coordinates.*

**FIGURE/GROUND**

*Some of the characteristics of composition have to do with such things as figure/ground relationships, negative and positive space, visual lines of force, and so on. These characteristics have more to do with perception than with what is literal in the picture. In the above drawing, we tend to attach more importance to the boats as a grouping of shapes than to the background, and therefore tend to separate the figures of the boats from the background in our minds. The composition itself is an illusion of space because we look at the boats, supposedly nearest us, first, then at the bridge in the middleground, and last our eyes are led into the distance by the perspective of the buildings in the background. Above and right we see the same drawing changed to emphasize first the figures of the boats, and then the background. Naturally, once the viewer has made note of this, the overall structure of the picture begins to fall into place. The boats, as shapes, point toward the left, but the eye is redirected into the drawing by the arching curve of the bridge, which is then caught by the vertical elements of tower and buildings. However, we must remember that the figure and background always interact and cannot be separated except for this sort of analysis.*

**POSITIVE AND NEGATIVE**

*The meaning of the terms positive and negative is related to photography but in painting and drawing they also have a more specific reference. While we show here an almost photographic negative reversal of the light and dark elements in this sketch we also refer by "positive" to the image of the object shown (in this case the sailboat) and by "negative" to the space around the object (the water, land, sky, etc.).*

**FULL AND EMPTY**

*Full and empty can have different meanings. In general, we consider the figures we see in the sketch above as "full" in as much as they have closed and compact forms; those in the second sketch as "empty" in as much as they have hollow, concave forms or ones drawn with a thin line. The concept concerns also the clustering together or dispersion of forms in a similar composition space.*

**REDUCTION TO SIMPLE FORMS**

*One method for beginning drawing mentioned on page 5 is to define the outlines of what you are to draw, and then draw the contours which describe important differences between areas. A helpful method which can prevent one from getting too lost in details of complicated contours is to turn the shapes you draw into geometric shapes rather than try to carefully follow actual contours at once. This involves roughly approximating the geometric shape that is nearest the one you are trying to draw, or just simplifying what you see into contour line. The left hand drawing in each pair below simplifies the drawing into two dimensional shapes, while each of those on the right suggests the three dimensional forms.*

## COMPOSITION AND SPACE

*Composition involves the arrangement in an apparent space of visual elements. Such elements are never completely independent of one another and relate to one another visually. Each such element takes up space, carves out its own territory, and groupings of them have their own identity. Knowing this permits the artist to have an impression of a whole that will be the total composition, before being concerned with the smaller elements of that composition.*

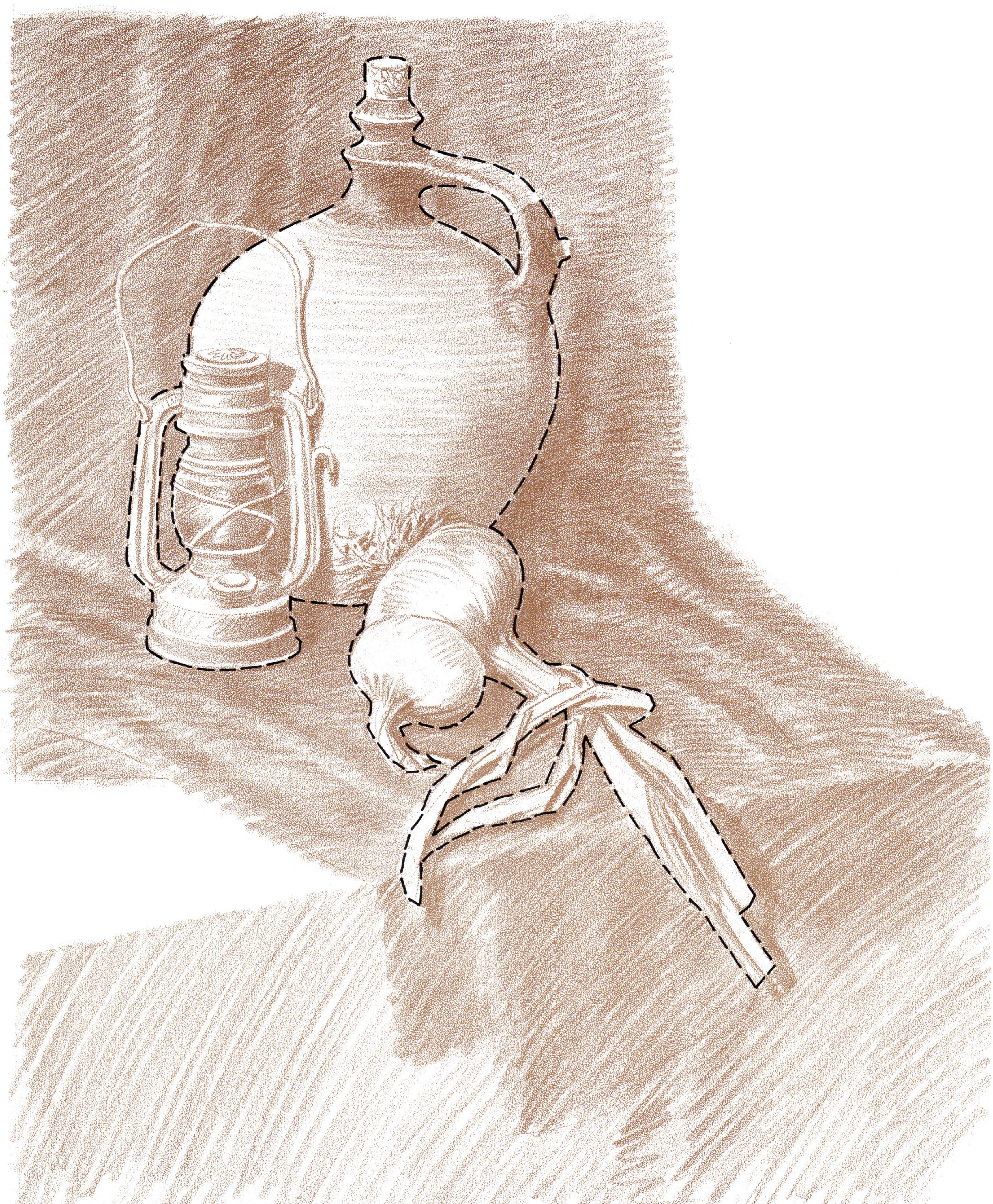

**ACTUAL SPACE AND GEOMETRIC SPACE**

*The illusion of space is an important concept for an artist to understand. For our purposes we mean by this not the space of "outer space" but rather the field-of-action as represented on the rectangular (usually) surface on which the artist draws or paints. In a literal scenic picture as at the bottom of the page, the artist must learn to control the illusion of foreground, middleground and background by the use of lines, overlapping, focus, etc. The upper sketches of geometric forms illustrate the illusion of three dimensions of objects, geometric or abstract forms.*

## THE FIELD OF INTERACTING FORCES

*Within our concept of geometric space we need to understand a field of interacting forces in which each element is taken not on its own but as a function of all the others. This space is the place in which the forms with their precise characteristics of contained tension, value, and light and shade are arranged in a given way to create the composition. It is the location of this coming together of all these elements and their consequent effect upon one another and thus upon the total picture that we call the field of interacting forces. What we are doing is controlling the fields of force which attract, repel, push and put the eye back and forth at any time between things that it sees.*

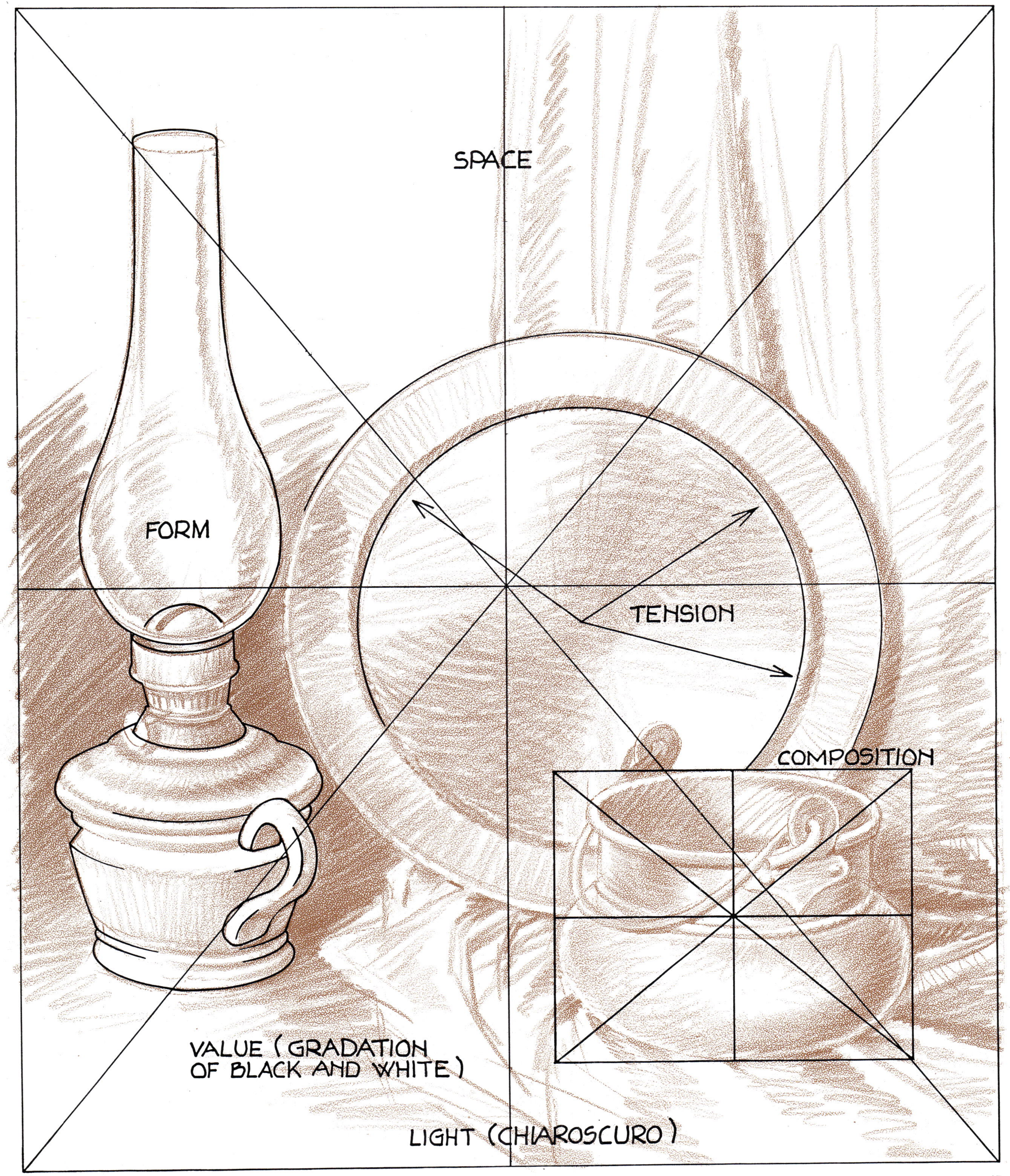

**VOLUME - PERSPECTIVE - CHIAROSCURO**

*In real space, everything three-dimensional we see has real volume: length, breadth, and height. It is our job as artists to create the illusion of these three dimensions on a two-dimensional surface. Perspective and chiaroscuro (light and shade) move the eye into and around a form which is itself an illusion. Volume five of this Leonardo series is wholly devoted to perspective and shadow. Since this is an important and detailed subject and because an understanding of perspective is such a practical tool for the artist, we refer the reader to this volume.*

*Likewise important, in order to give plasticity and relief to the elements of a composition, is chiaroscuro, which can be soft and delicate in an atmosphere of half lights and penumbra, but can also reach effects of great force and drama in full light, with very dense and clear projection of shadow. The effective distribution of highlight and shadow is the key to chiaroscuro.*

**LIGHT**

*Light is a fundamental element of a drawing which defines all possible spatial relationships (full and empty, light and dark, contrast, etc.). We can consider it to modulate form in a picture and also understand that the forms that are shown themselves modulate light. There is an obvious connection between chiaroscuro and light. Light, as a term, means both the degree of illumination and the sources of direction of that illumination. It is defined in many ways by highlights, by cast shadows, and by the clarity of definition and the contrast of value with which the forms are defined.*

**LIGHT**
*In this illustration, the drawings on the left of each similar pair are drawn as though seen under an unusually flat-lit situation and although we see by their geometry that the shapes are supposed to be three-dimensional, their even illumination deprives us of shadow information. The drawings on the right, however, are drawn as though they are illuminated under strong oblique lighting as a main source, and so are richly modeled. The darkness and lightness of the grey is known as its value.*

# The Color

To say color and to say light is the same thing, as will be illustrated later on this page. But to understand what this means to the painter, it will be enough to say that he carries out his work by means of color, that color is his specific means of expression whatever may be the technique he uses. The world in which we live has an infinite variety of forms, all of them always covered in countless colors; and the close connection between shapes and colors presented to us by reality is found by us in all the history of painting. Of course, the manner of interpreting and resolving this connection varies in detail from artist to artist, and more in general terms from age to age. There have always been schools and "trends" in which we can place individual personalities, setting in relief the elements which they have in common; and controversies have always arisen between the various trends. The most important opposition, however, is that which took place in the second half of the last century, with the impressionist revolution, and which marked a sharp turning-point in what was meant by color. On this subject, through lack of space, we would refer the reader to our volume no. 25 Still Life, which also shows what is said about color and colors in other numbers; and instead we will attempt to explain here what is color as a natural phenomenon, that is the color-light identity.

If we observe a small beam of light going through a prism, we see the "spectrum" appear: we also see the splitting-up of light into a series of colors, which go from red to violet, passing through orange, yellow, green, and blue.

We "see" the external world and perceive colors and shapes by means of the eyes, which behave exactly like a camera the iris acts as a diaphragm and the crystalline lens as an adaptable lens (objective), the retina as a film onto which is projected the image inverted and then righted once again. Then the image is carried to the brain by the optic nerve, where the mysterious process takes place which comes to light as "vision".

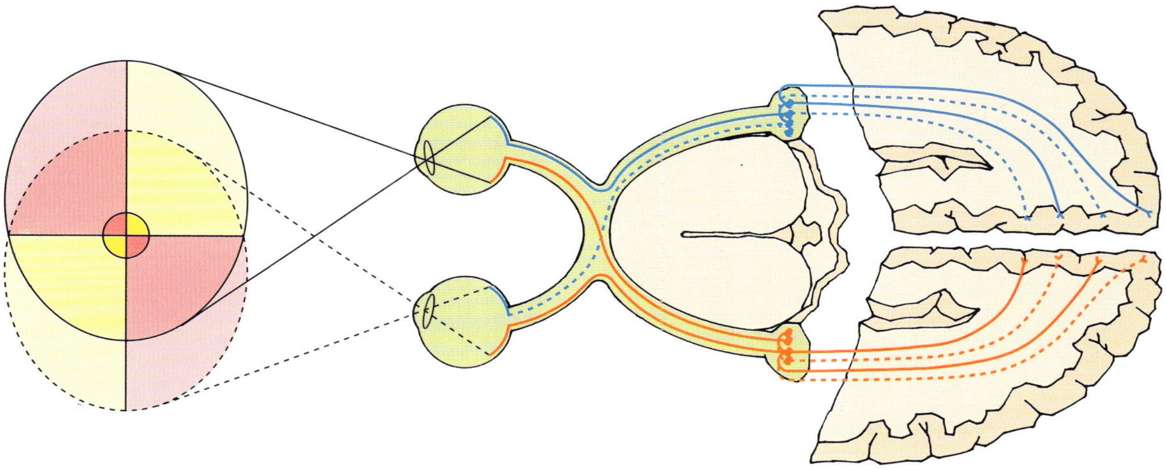

Light is nothing more than the visible part of electromagnetic radiation, which goes from the longest radio waves to the ultrashort X or gamma rays or cosmic rays. Wavelengths between 687 and 397 microns (thousandths of mm), make up the spectrum and are visible as colors. Colors therefore are a property of light; and when we say that a given surface is red, we mean that it reflects the wavelength of red and absorbs all the others. To observe colors (the human eye can distinguish thousands) means discovering the fascinating play of light on the things of this world.

*If we choose and isolate red, yellow and blue from the solar spectrum, we shall get the three primary colors: they are fundamental, because they can give, when mixed correctly, all other colors. The mixing is valid not only optically but also materially with all types of colors generally used by painters. By mixing red and yellow we obtain orange, from yellow and blue we get green and from red and blue we get violet: three important secondary colors, each of which is complementary to the primary color excluded from the mixture. In a painting, the juxtaposition of a primary and its complementary (for example, red and green) makes the two colors "throb" in a strange way, as if they were trying to mix without succeeding when mixed together, they in fact "calm down" in a sort of grey. Even the mixture of the three primary colors in equal parts gives grey. However proceeding in the schematic combinations illustrated on this page, we obtain the tertiary colors; we can go ahead as we wish, always with new colors to consider as "pure". Pure colors are those which are the result of mixing one or two primary colors and their derivatives, excluding the third primary and its derivatives, impure colors are those made from two of the primary colors and a little of the third. To single out a progressive series of mixtures which will always give pure colors, the chromatic circle, an example of which we give in reduced size on the opposite page, will be useful. In this circle all the colors are pure and the union of contiguous colors always produces new colors which are pure likewise.*

*Leonardo technical manuals*

# THE HORSE

*Anatomy plates for artists*

PUBLISHED BY VINCIANA

*Leonardo technical manuals*

# HUMAN ANATOMY

*Anatomy plates for artists*

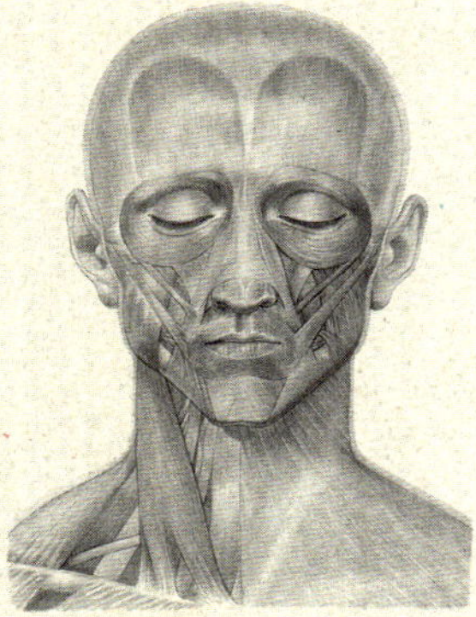

PUBLISHED BY VINCIANA

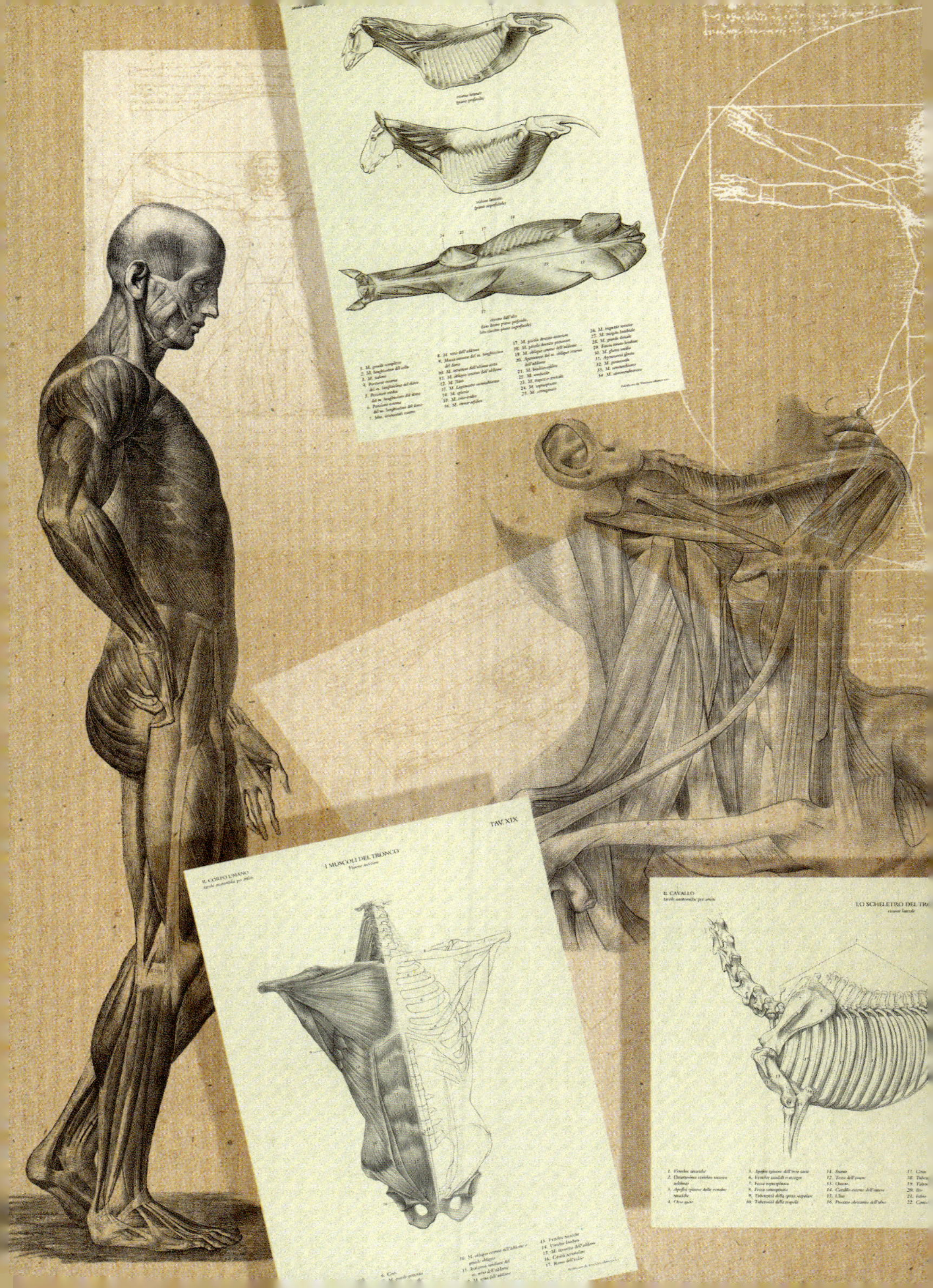

TAV. XIX
I MUSCOLI DEL TRONCO
IL CORPO UMANO
IL CAVALLO
LO SCHELETRO DEL TR

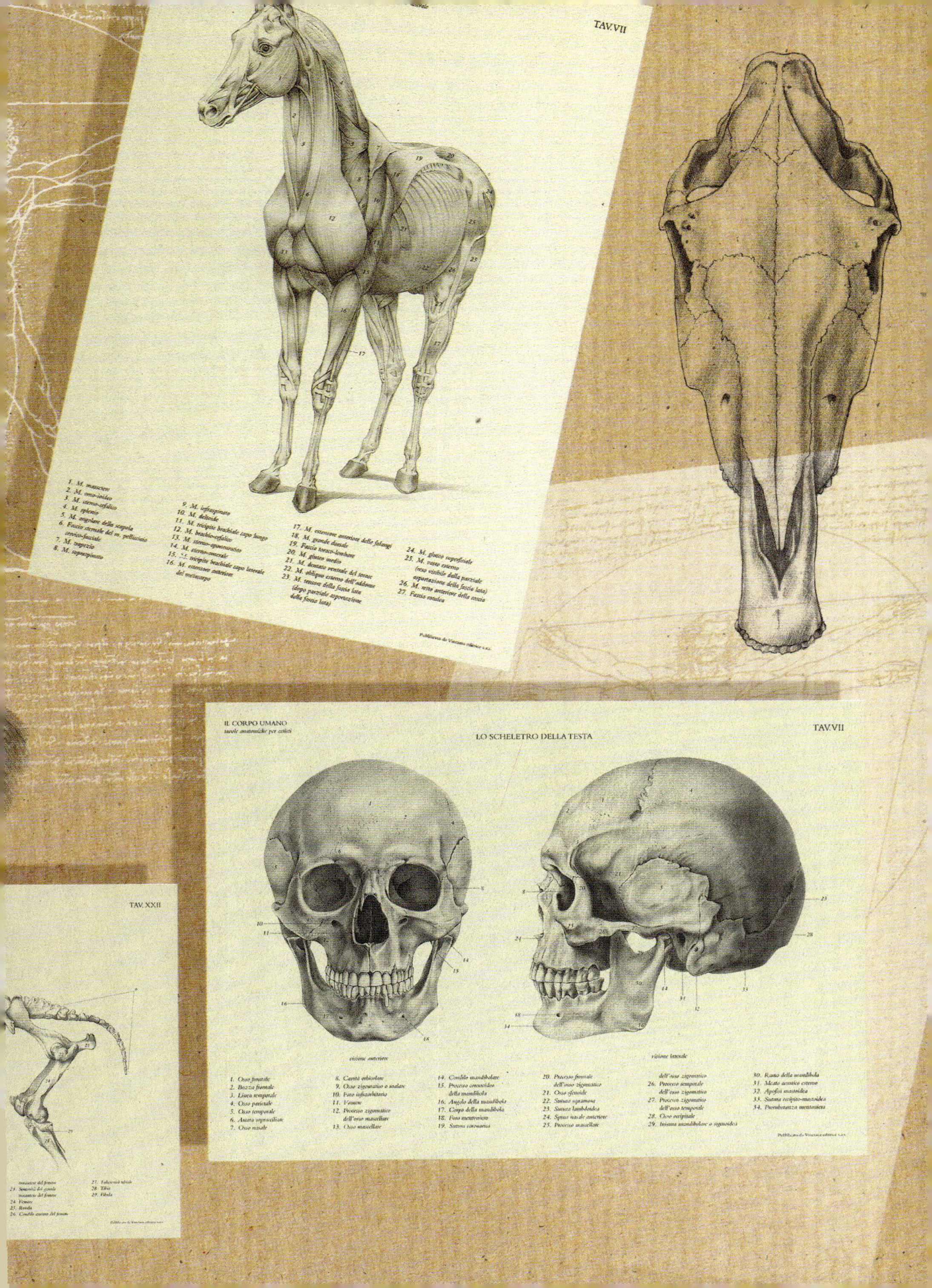

TAV.VII
1. M. massetere
2. M. omo-ioideo
3. M. sterno-cefalico
4. M. splenio
5. M. angolare della scapola
6. Fascio sternale del m. pellicciaio cervico-facciale
7. M. trapezio
8. M. sopraspinato
9. M. infraspinato
10. M. deltoide
11. M. tricipite brachiale capo lungo
12. M. brachio-cefalico
13. M. sterno-aponeurotico
14. M. sterno-omerale
15. M. tricipite brachiale capo laterale
16. M. estensore anteriore del metacarpo
17. M. estensore anteriore delle falangi
18. M. grande dorsale
19. Fascia toraco-lombare
20. M. gluteo medio
21. M. dentato ventrale del torace
22. M. obliquo esterno dell'addome
23. M. tensore della fascia lata (dopo parziale asportazione della fascia lata)
24. M. gluteo superficiale
25. M. vasto esterno (reso visibile dalla parziale asportazione della fascia lata)
26. M. retto anteriore della coscia
27. Fascia rotulea
IL CORPO UMANO
tavole anatomiche per artisti
LO SCHELETRO DELLA TESTA
TAV.VII
visione anteriore
visione laterale
1. Osso frontale
2. Bozza frontale
3. Linea temporale
4. Osso parietale
5. Osso temporale
6. Arcata sopraccilliare
7. Osso nasale
8. Cavità orbicolare
9. Osso zigomatico o malare
10. Foro infraorbitario
11. Vomere
12. Processo zigomatico dell'osso mascellare
13. Osso mascellare
14. Condilo mandibolare
15. Processo coronoideo della mandibola
16. Angolo della mandibola
17. Corpo della mandibola
18. Foro mentoniero
19. Sutura coronarica
20. Processo frontale dell'osso zigomatico
21. Osso sfenoide
22. Sutura squamosa
23. Sutura lambdoidea
24. Spina nasale anteriore
25. Processo mascellare dell'osso zigomatico
26. Processo temporale dell'osso zigomatico
27. Processo zigomatico dell'osso temporale
28. Osso occipitale
29. Incisura mandibolare o sigmoidea
30. Ramo della mandibola
31. Meato acustico esterno
32. Apofisi mastoidea
33. Sutura occipito-mastoidea
34. Protuberanza mentoniera
TAV. XXII
24. Femore
28. Tibia
29. Fibula

After 20 years in the field of drawing and painting through publication of the Leonardo Collection, Vinciana Publishing has decided to utilise its vast experience by inaugurating a new line of anatomical volumes from an artistic perspective commencing with volumes devoted to the anatomy of the horse and the human body. These volumes have a unique special appearance, inspired by anatomy texts from the late nineteenth century. Each volume consists of 48 loose plates plus an instructional text. The structure of the volume permits readers to use the individual plates without the restrictions imposed by bindings; for example, one can put two plates side by side - whether these illustrate the head, the thorax, or another part - and compare bone structure to muscle structure. Each plate is numbered and indicates both the part illustrated and its scientific nomenclature. Consequently the use of the plates is independent from the text, and reading is a choice left to those who would like to improve their knowledge of anatomy. The designs, which unfold step by step along with the text, start with the parts of the head, move on to the trunk, and end with the front and hind limbs. The bone structure and the muscle structure is examined for each part of the body. Most of the illustrations printed on the 48 plates has been drawn entirely by ballpoint pen, using a patient technique that has borne excellent results especially in the representation of muscles.

Just as light can be split up into various wavelengths (or colors), so the colors can be put together again, that is added together all at once or partly. We could say, to be clear, that the addition of colors tends towards white, while taking colors away leads towards black, as shown in the two synthesis schemes of primary colors which we show here. We can make a test, for example for additive synthesis, by putting red glass on top of blue glass: we will see that the resulting color (magenta) is appreciably lighter than either red or blue. If then we put all three primary colors on top of each other with the addition of yellow glass, there will be absolutely no color to see, if we look through the pieces of glass. On the other hand, practically all the colors used by painters are examples of subtractive synthesis, because they are made up of substances "reflecting" a given color, with the exclusion or reduction to the minimum of "absorbent" substances. As for black and white mentioned above, it will be useful to remember that they are net colors, but the sum and absence respectively of all the colors. Besides, in nature absolute black and absolute white are very rare; and it is advisable that they should be used as little as possible in painting also.

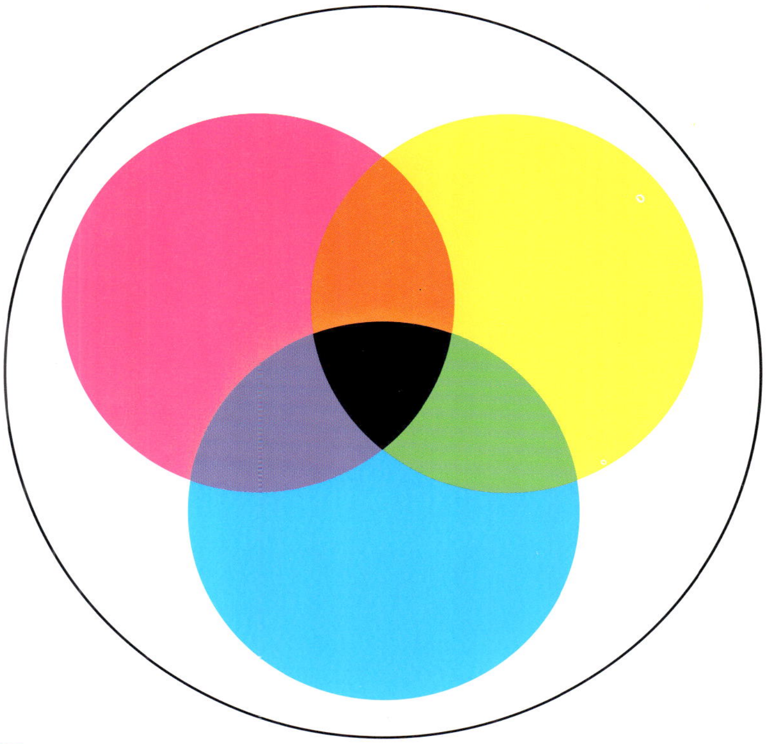

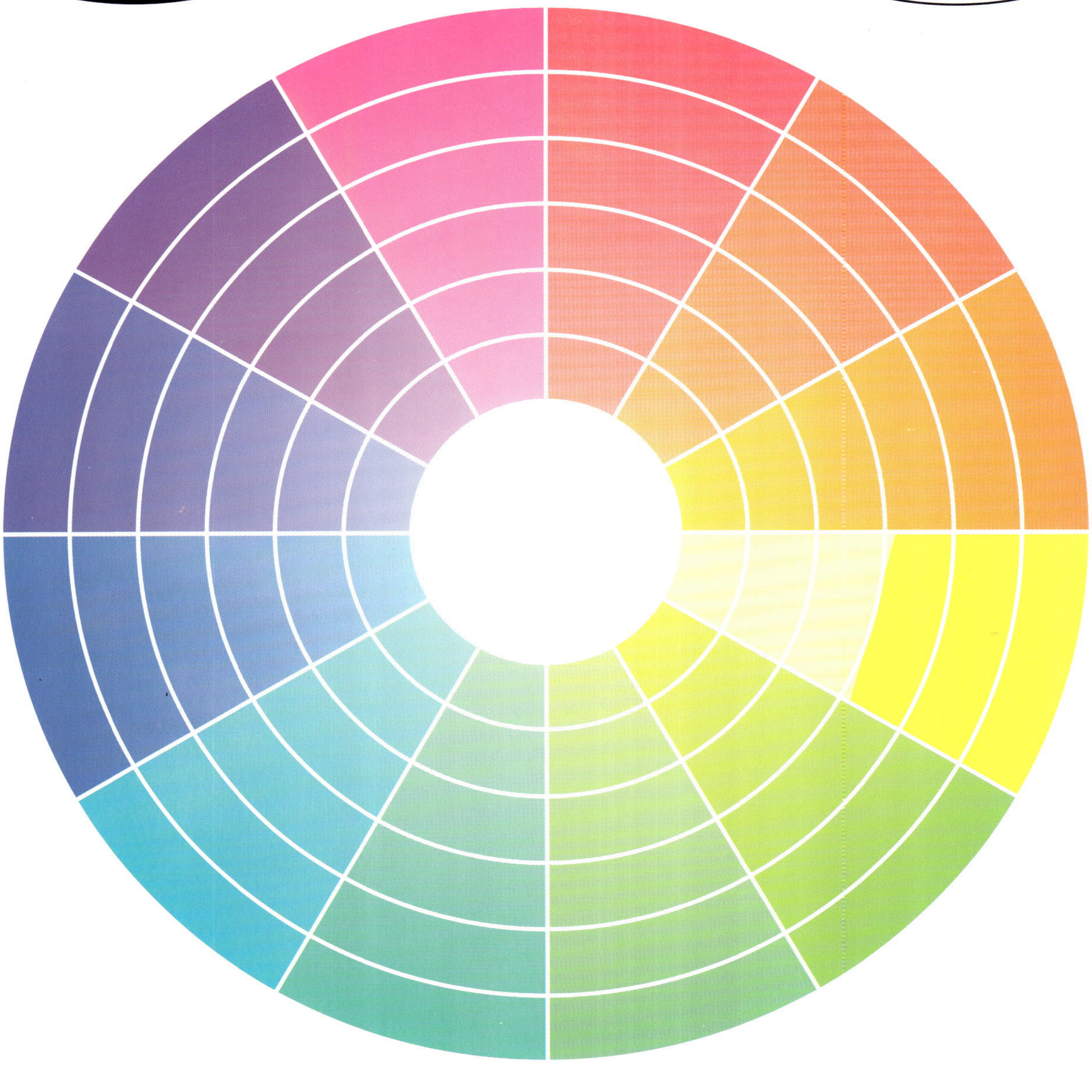

*Here we give a table showing the colors which come from mixing two colors in equal parts, beginning with a series of twelve. The resulting color is found, as in the multiplication tables, at the meeting-point of the vertical and the horizontal referring to the two colors to be mixed. The squares considered are 12x12=144, but the effective combinations are 66; in fact, these combinations are repeated on one side and on the other of the diagonal which starts from the top left, while the 12 colors which stand on the diagonal itself are the same as the colors started with. The original of the table was in watercolor but it is obvious that this scheme is valid for any type of colors one might want to use.*

**LIGHT SOURCE**

*Two types of light sources are important for the artist; the light falling upon the subject matter being drawn or painted and the illumination on the actual canvas or board or other material on which the artist works. Light on the subject generally depends on an invisible source which stands outside the picture: to the left, to the right, behind the observer (as is shown here below), or in any other position including the front, that is, facing the light. The choice of one type of light source or another is open, but it must always be made in relation to the results which we want to obtain: plastic relief with volumes which stand out and sharp contrasts, or a tonal atmosphere based on soft and harmonious parts, or something which is to be found more or less between one or the other. As an artist works, the best position for someone who is drawing on a more or less inclined surface is when the light comes from high up on the left with an inclination of 45°: in this case, in fact, the shadow cast by the hand always leaves free the part of the drawing which is being blocked out at the time. It is well to remember this if working in an enclosed room with strong direct light or in the open with the sun; while it is much less important in indirect light or when the sky is overcast.*

*In a naturalistic scene as the building shown here you must remember that because the light source is the sun, the time of day and its consequent meanings, moods, romantic allusions, etc. can also be implied or conveyed.*

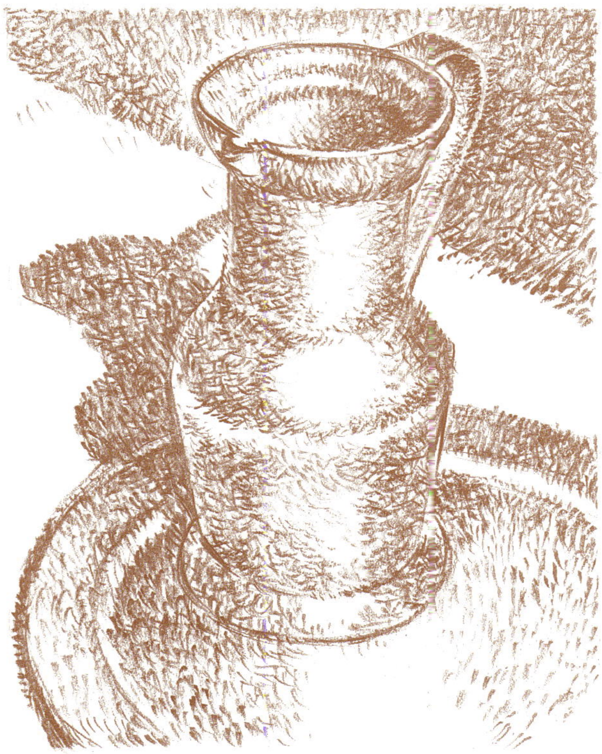

**CHIAROSCURO TECHNIQUES**

*Chiaroscuro can be achieved in a large number of ways which are all different, and all allowable where they satisfy a minimum of stylistic coherence and are not, as is commonly said, "messy". A good rule is that of never completely blending the strokes in shading and tracts, using the fingers or stumps; the latter should be avoided in any case. If the first of the examples shown here is observed well, it will be seen that the hatching is so carefully blended that on first sight it is almost indistinguishable, and yet we can, for the greater part at least, still make out the direction of the stroke. The other drawings (looking from left to right and from top to bottom) present uniformly diagonal hatching, crossed hatching in groups, vertical hatching in bands of strokes, pointillist hatching and finally coarse and rather granular hatching.*

**ATMOSPHERIC PERSPECTIVE**

*Now let us look for a while at this tree landscape, divided by a stream of water which goes away towards the horizon. To give the feeling of depth, as well as the correct construction due to the linear perspective, there is something further, and that is atmospheric perspective. Leonardo called it "aerial perspective", and for him it was the variation of the density and color of the air, according to the variation of distance. Not having color here, the artist has cleverly gauged the range of greys and lessened - as he (gradually) goes away from the foreground in depth - the incisiveness of the stroke. Taking atmospheric perspective into account means, in brief, giving the feeling of the air which circulates between each of the perspective planes.*

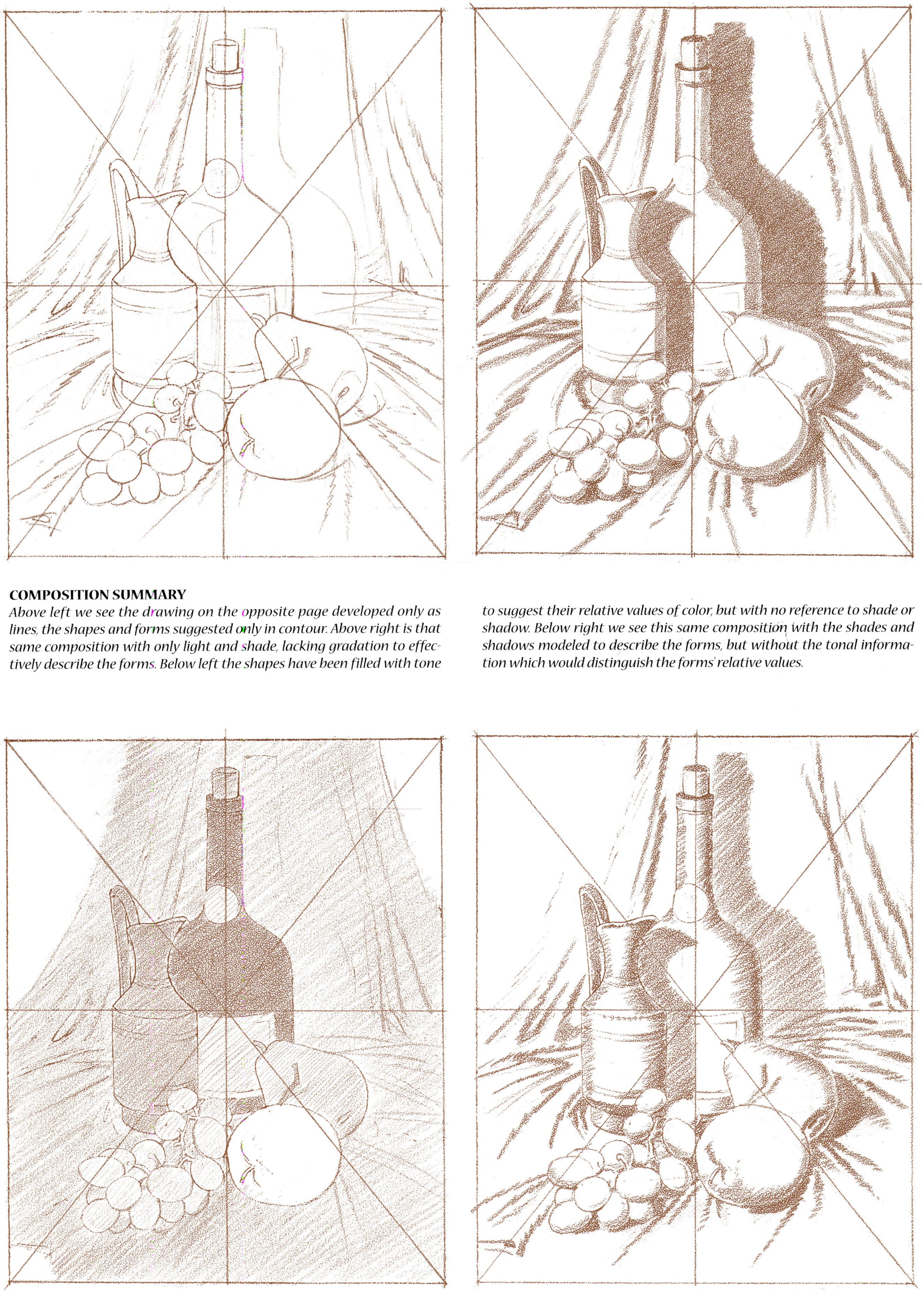

**COMPOSITION SUMMARY**

*Above left we see the drawing on the opposite page developed only as lines, the shapes and forms suggested only in contour. Above right is that same composition with only light and shade, lacking gradation to effectively describe the forms. Below left the shapes have been filled with tone to suggest their relative values of color, but with no reference to shade or shadow. Below right we see this same composition with the shades and shadows modeled to describe the forms, but without the tonal information which would distinguish the forms' relative values.*

**DEVELOPED COMPOSITION**

*In this drawing we have all four kinds of information summarized on the preceding page: contour, light and shade, tone and modeling. To understand composition, however, we must also examine how elements are arranged in a field, and explore the available choices and judgements.*

## EQUILIBRIUM AND DISEQUILIBRIUM

*Equilibrium means the state of rest or stability. In a composition with only one dominant element the degree of equilibrium depends on its position in the space. If there are several objects competing for dominance, then their degree of equilibrium will depend both on their positions in the space, and on their relative positions with respect to one another. Balance is a simpler term for equilibrium, like children on a seesaw. It should be said that disequilibrium may still be utilized if it works in the totality of the whole.*

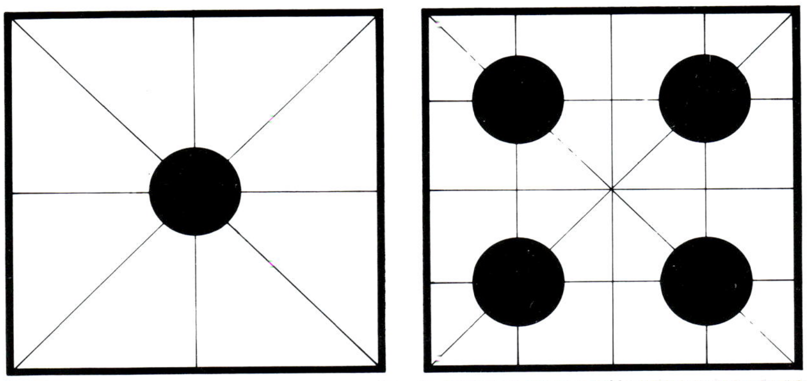

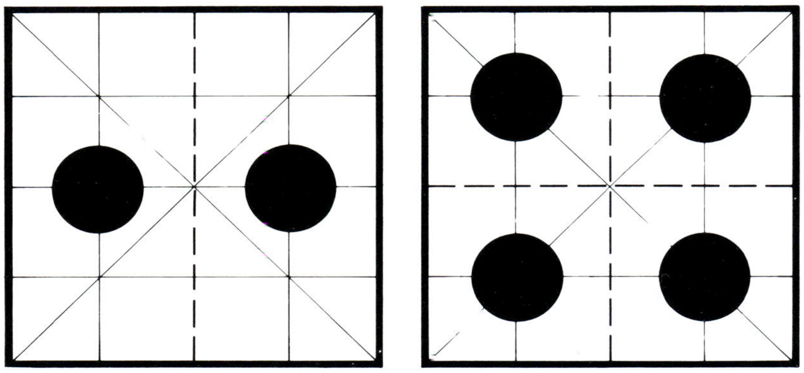

## SYMMETRY AND ASYMMETRY

*A symmetrical composition consists of approximately equal balance of elements on either side of a vertical or horizontal axis or both. Symmetry usually results in a formal composition. Asymmetry relies for its balance upon an unequal distribution of the size or location of visual elements and arrives at visual harmony without the use of a "mirror image" composition.*

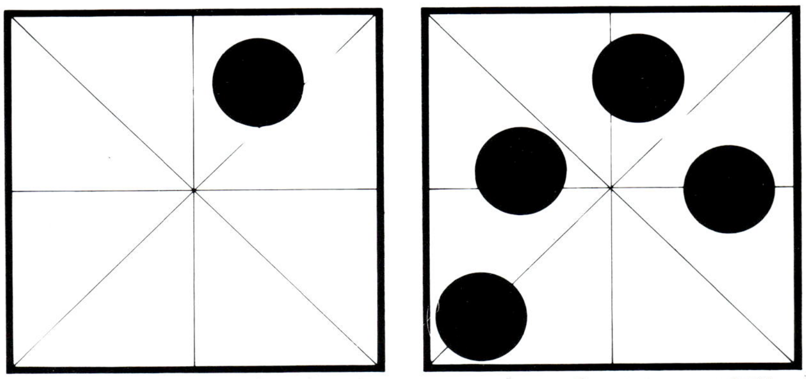

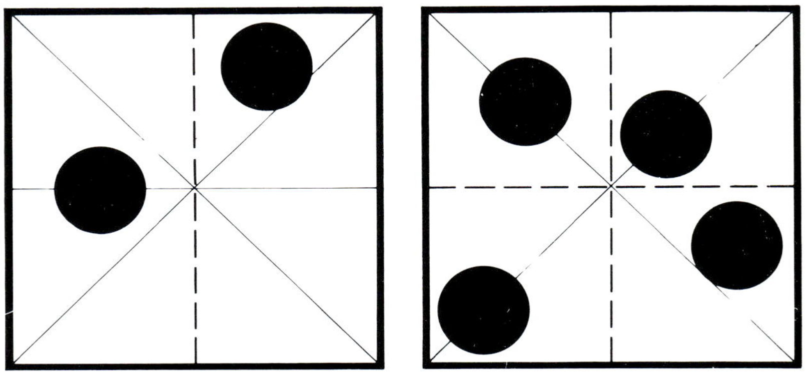

## WEIGHT

*Weight is the force exercised by a body (or a group of bodies) on what acts as its support, because of the earth's force of gravity. Weight and equilibrium are often closely connected, because equilibrium can also be defined as an "equalling of weight"; weight is also related to mass, that is the quantity of material contained in a body. The concepts of weight, mass and equilibrium come to us from physics, and, of course, hold true in the field of composition too, but it must not be forgotten that this field is one of appearance, visual representations, not reality. Visually, for example, the weight of a bunch of flowers like the one sketched below, is much greater than the weight of the same flowers in reality.*

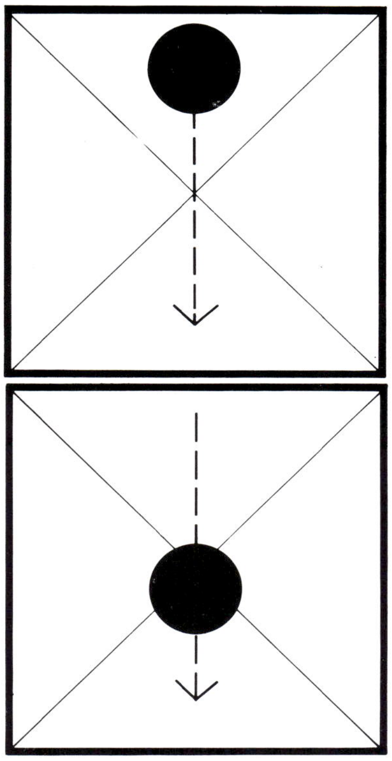

## REVERSED IMAGE

*It would appear that an image reversed from left to right or vice versa (mirror image), ought to appear identical and so have the same effect on us; however, it is not so. Apart from its first impact with the image, the eye usually tends to "read" it from left to right, as it does with writing, so that in the first subject below, for instance, the imagination seeks to enlarge the picture beyond the limit cropping off the flowers, the shadow and the base while in the second, the mirror image, the cropping is a precise starting point and nothing else. The first is more "evocative" than the second.*

## THE CROPPING OF THE PICTURE

*The word cropping comes from the terminology used in photographic technique and means as much the choice of the shot with the exclusion of what is not of interest, as the actual cropping of a frame to reduce it to the essentials. The first meaning holds true in painting and drawing - the meaning of the choice of the limits of the picture. In the subject on this page, the four different croppings are seen for the difference in effect they can produce.*

## COMPOSITIONAL PLANS

*Space, form, light, value (tones of grey), chiaroscuro, volume, and then equilibrium and disequilibrium, symmetry, weight etc.... all this, and more besides, comes together to create a composition, and is a sum of elements which are always present. The placing in space of the forms and the relative configuration of all the other elements clearly gives rise to an infinite number of solutions, and it is not possible to describe even a part of them. What we can do is give some examples of still life, marking on top of them a few lines which show, in a general way, the constructive plan, and give a short explanatory comment on each.*

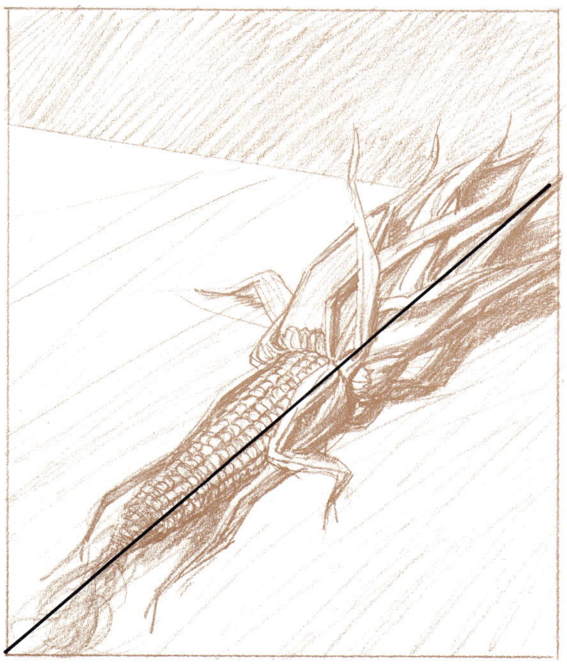

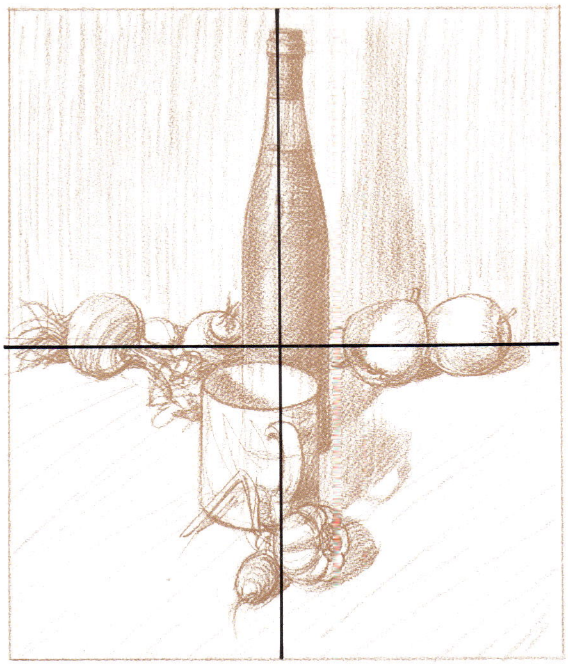

*1) Reversed T plan, centralized bilateral symmetry. The figure, which is initially static, acquires an upward movement from the background.*
*2) Bilateral symmetry obtained with a U plan, where the background is almost flat and accentuates the central division between the bottle and the lamp.*
*3) Pyramid plan, in which the light asymmetry of the left is compensated by the obliqueness of the sharp edge of the light of the background. A feeling of peace and concentration.*
*4) L plan, decisively asymmetric, which immediately gives an idea of movement. The empty obscurity of the background seems to draw the candlestick and the book towards it.*
*5) Diagonal plan, dynamic in itself in spite of the evident fixedness of an apparently accidental composition.*
*6) Quadripartite symmetry. A static arrangement as far as the figure is concerned, while the background moves with radially diverging light and shadows.*

**STATIC COMPOSITIONS**

*The question of the static or dynamic property of a composition is rather complex, as can be understood easily, in as much as it is the result of many pre-existing causes which cannot be singled out easily. The equation "equilibrium = static state" is certainly valid, but only as a general rule. Look at the three compositions on this page, which appear very well-balanced in mass, volume and chiaroscuro, on a basis of perfect bilateral symmetry; there is also the physical equilibrium (that is the perfect stability) of the objects taken one by one, and there is a well-balanced distribution of light and shadows. They are, therefore, static compositions. Now look at the opposite page.*

**DYNAMIC COMPOSITIONS**

*Here we have repeated the three previous subjects, varying the placement of the elements and the perspective, and in this way we have moved on to asymmetric compositions, where the evidence of tension has taken the place of equilibrium. Now these compositions are dynamic: the first, because of the sliding of the figure group to the right side, the second because of the lively rearrangement of the flowers, the third because of moving to an angled view. Nevertheless it is essential to note that classification never has an absolute value.*

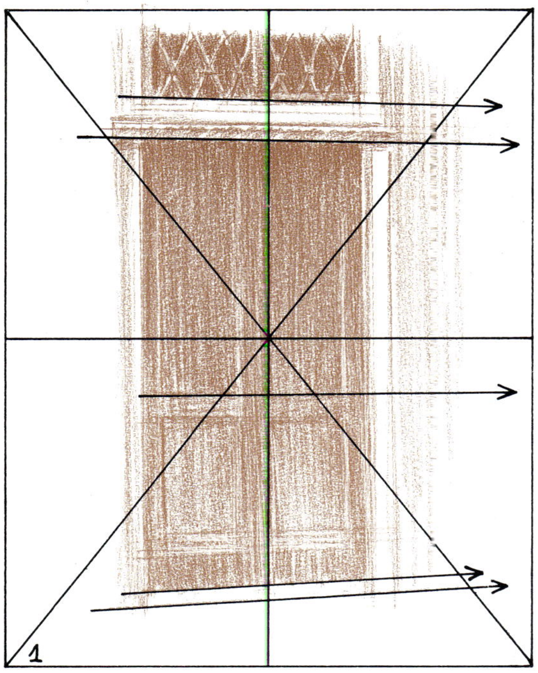


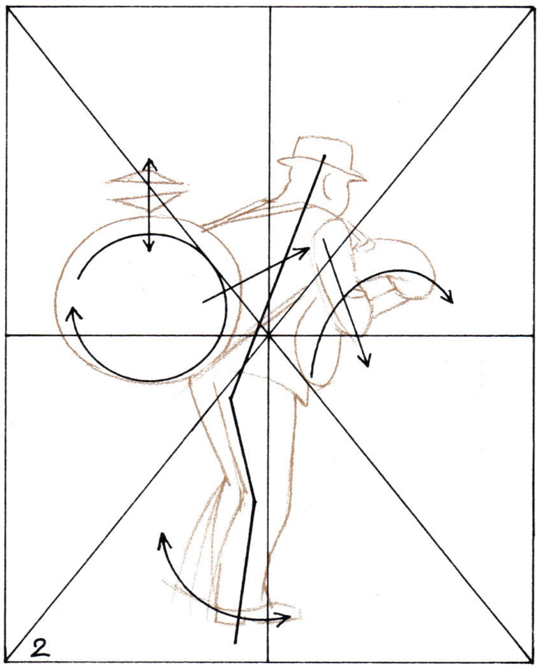


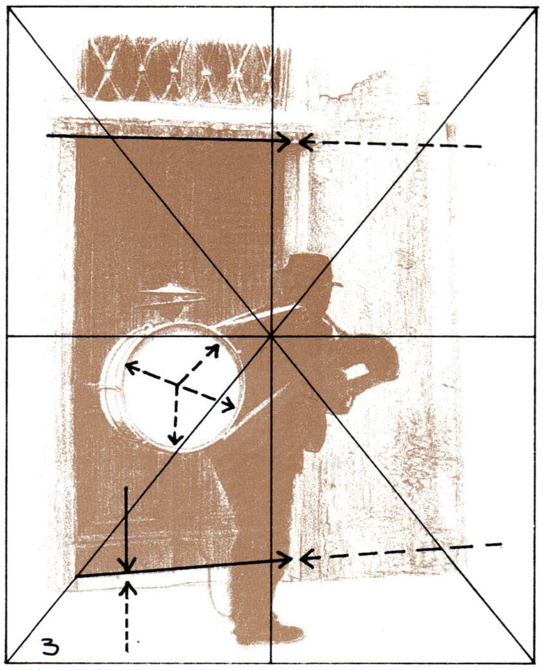

**TENSION AND COMPRESSION**

*Tension is the strain of things pulling apart. New suspension bridges work on the basis of tension. The lines of tension are the cables that strain between the high pilings and the weight of the bridge itself. Compression is the crushing together of those same forces. Old stone bridges push their weight, stone after stone, into one another and eventually into the ground. The lines of force are often visible in the arched openings between the load-bearing stones. Since the artist is an illusionist, a drawing is also a set of illusions of tension and compression. Where visual forces are strung out against one another, there is tension, and where those forces crush into one another, there is compression. In the drawing of the street musician to the left there are many tensions and compressions. Some of the major ones are: 1)perspective - 2) directions within the figure - 3) tension and contrast between dark and light masses - 4) relation of figure to ground.*

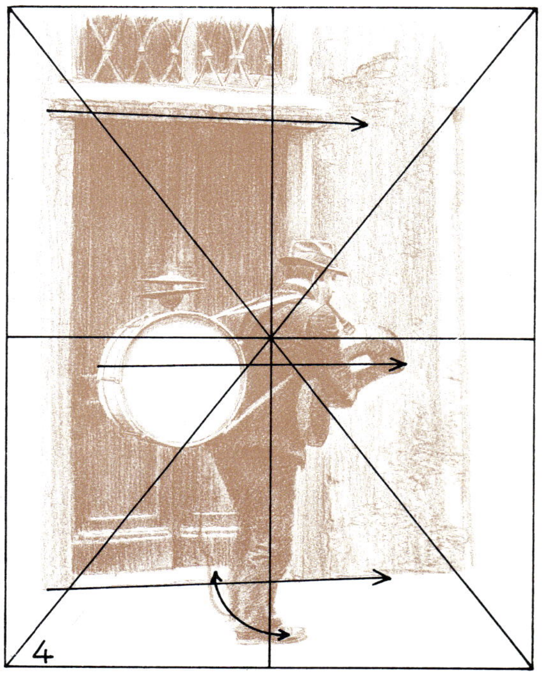

**ELEMENTS OF TENSION AND COMPRESSION**

*The elements of design all interact with one another along this dimension of tension and compression. Line, shape, form, color, texture all contrast in this way. Depending on how you look at a work, and which shifting complexes of forces you attend to, the tensions and compressions change according to 1) the line - 2) the form - 3) the composition - 4) the light.*

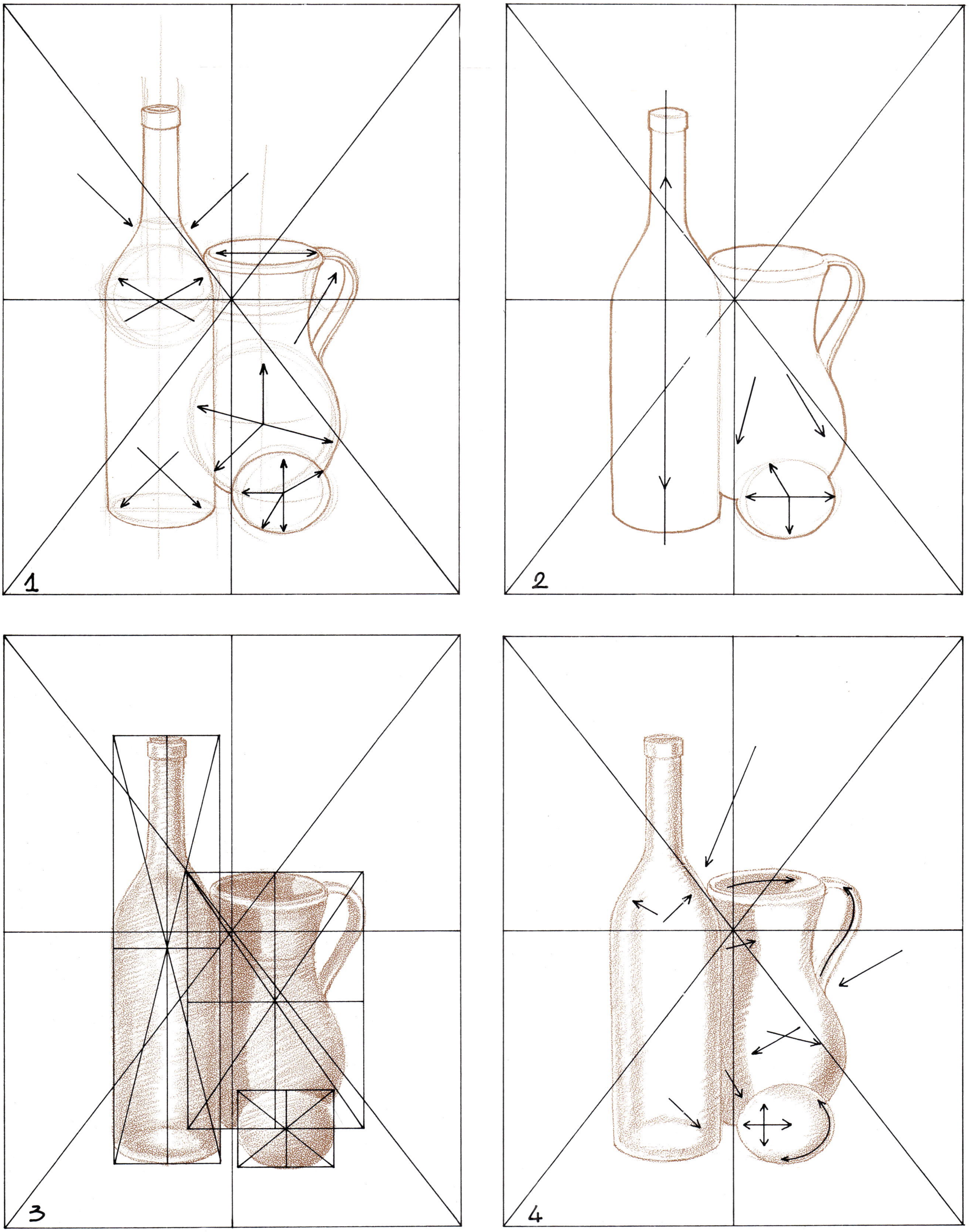

**MOVEMENT**

*The purpose of the person who makes use of tensions to make a dynamic composition is to give the illusion of movement. But there is another way also, borrowed from the technique of the cinema, which achieves surprising results. It involves the use of "sequence", an example of which we give below in a series of six moving drawings; the last is only the superimposition of the previous ones. Sequence, as you know, is the basis of animated drawing. It divides movement into a well-accentuated rhythmic series where the succession of movements (the frames to be projected) is outlined on a surface with a modular structure: that is, the changes are calculated on a modular scheme which acts as an invisible support to the surrounding drawing. Of course, movement implies direction and the artist controls both at the same time as he or she makes the eye follow along.*

## EXPRESSION

*Practical examples of expression are given in the drawings below. Each of the three subjects has been dealt with in a different expressive manner, marked by the formal use of light or violent chiaroscuro, continuous or broken strokes, close or spaced hatching, soft or harshly contrasted tonal graduation, etc. Clearly, individual sensitivity to these differences determines the choices that an artist makes, and thus, the techniques that are used. The goal of these choices is to better convey some of the differences of mood, feeling, and impact that the drawing can have.*

## EXPRESSION

*The drawings shown below suggest that an artist, with some practice and control of technique, may lend to his or her drawings a great deal of emotional content. Indeed, the way that an artist perceives the world around him can be an individual and highly personal observation that is reflected in the nature of the works of art that are produced. We suggest that you first approach the drawing of "real" things in a craftsman-like manner to learn to control the elements in a drawing. You will then be able to better control the "expressiveness" of your interpretations of these things when you are no longer a beginner.*